Times Past

A
31-Day Devotional
of
Psalms, Poetry, Power, Prayer & Praise

by Theresa C. Allen

Times Past
A
31-Day Devotional
of
Psalms, Poetry, Power, Prayer & Praise

Copyright © 2000
Allen's Ink Publishing Company
First Printing - November 2000

Published by: Allen's Ink Publishing Company
allens_ink@yahoo.com

Cover by: D. Brown Designs.....Art with an Attitude

ISBN: 0-9676710-1-9

Printed in the United States by:
Morris Publishing
3212 East Highway 30
Kearney, NE 68847
1-800-650-7888

Dedication....

To my husband

Leonard Lewis Allen, Sr.

For listening endlessly
to every thought I
have ever written, and for enduring
patiently as I smoothed out the edges.
I am eternally grateful for your continual
belief in me, and for an awesome title for
this book.

For being the gift of my past,
the joy of my present,
and the promise of my future,
I thank you.

I will always love you!
T.

iv

Acknowledgments

"Let love and faithfulness never leave you;
bind them around your neck, write them on
the tablet of your heart."
(Proverbs 3:3)

I have read that "A poem is not finished until it is published, and then it is still subject to change." *(author unknown)*

Another book, and the Author and Finisher of my faith gets all the praise!

To the King of Kings and the Lord of Lords in my life, thanks for putting poetry in *"The Book,"* and consequently planting it in my heart. This is evidence of your divine power. For without you this would not – could not have been possible.

To my kids: Leonard Jr., and Laniya, you have added much joy to my life. It is my hope that you are forever reminded to never give up on faith, hope or love. Know that the greatest of all these is love.

To my dear friend, Pam. If "Thank Yous" were money you would have more money than you could possibly spend in this lifetime. I thank you for again believing in a dream that was brought to life because of your faithfulness to see it through. I thank you for encouraging, editing, and not allowing your faith to fail as we both wait on the promise of Him. You have been a great source of strength for me and I know that Heaven will someday reward you all that you are truly due. Love always...

To Delven: Another great cover! Some say, "you cannot judge a book by the cover." They would be wrong. Thank you for capturing the "Power and Praise" contained in this book. You have dressed "Times Past" very nicely. I cannot wait to see what you will do next. May the blessings of God overtake you!

To a dear friend from the past, Barbara. Midway through the writing of this book, the Spirit of God led me to a book you gave me in 1992. The words inscribed inside the jacket were: "One day I'll see your book of poems in a book much like this." My friend, here it is. Thank you for speaking forth in 1992 what God would birth in 2000.

To all of you who have been faithful readers over the years, (many of whom have watched my writing grow through the Ministry of *"The Christian Connection,"*) thank you for being a part of a past that I will always remember.

And to you who allow the message of "Times Past" to rest in your spirit, I am tremendously honored and humbled that you hold our book in your hands. May you find the comfort in reading it that I found while writing it.

From My Heart to Yours...

Introduction....

Everyday we all need a jump-start to
focus, reflect, and press through the various
issues of day-to-day life.
"Times Past" has exactly what you need!

It comprises poetry from a time that
would long be forgotten, had it not been for
the pages of this book.

Each day we have provided a personal "Praise Page"
so that you, too, can record some thoughts
that should never be forgotten.

This month I share with you thoughts worth
remembering, and I pray these thoughts minister
to you when and where you need it the most.

As you go through, day after day,
I hope you are lifted, inspired, and encouraged.

May "Times Past" propel you through the worst of
times and celebrate your best of times.
With each passing day, may God be glorified!

Times Past

A
31-Day Devotional
of
Psalms, Poetry, Power, Prayer & Praise

Today's Power Phrase

If You Follow

Where He Leads You

You Will Find

His Grace

Will Keep

You

Times Past

Day 1

Direct my footsteps according to your word;
let no sin rule over me.
(Psalms 119:133)

In the hustle and hurry of the morning we wake up, bathe, get dressed, get our coffee, and out the door we go. Some things we routinely forget, but before we leave the house we MUST remember to stop and pray.

There is so much to do today that we cannot afford to start the day off wrong. Lack of focus makes us prey to the daily, "devil delays." The devil is looking to interrupt your minute, mess up your hour, and devastate your day.

Prayer is the key to your daily success.
The prayer of your heart need not be long, but it must be prayed if you want it to be heard.

Spend your morning in fellowship with Christ.
He is your defense against the enemy.

Take this moment and seek the Lord in prayer.
May His power in Heaven and on earth guide your thoughts and actions today.

My Prayer Today

Lord, as I go about this day
I seek to do your will,
and trod the road in which I'll see
my destiny fulfilled.

As I go from place to place
allow the world to see
that I am never alone,
but that You walk along with me.

Help me to go with courage,
walking in boldness, speaking of You.
Let nothing hinder the work
You have anointed my hands to do.

If I stumble, fail or falter,
Lord, remind me, if You please,
that my success is found in You,
the giver of great and mighty things.

Keep my mind from thinking evil.
Help my motives remain pure.
Let each challenge bring forth a victory
and may the accolades all be Yours.

"Personal Praise Page"

_____

_____

_____

_____

_____

_____

_____

_____

_____

_____

_____

_____

_____

_____

_____

_____

Today's Power Phrase

The

Smallest Gestures

Can Make

The Biggest

Differences

Times Past

Day 2

Give thanks to the Lord, for He is good;
His love endures forever.
(Psalms 107:1)

There are many times throughout our day that we
consciously say,
"Thanks."
We thank the newspaper carrier for the morning
paper. At the office, we thank the person who
arrived first and made the coffee. At the bank, we
thank the teller for giving us our money. At the
grocery store, we thank the person who bagged
our groceries. At the doctor's office, we thank the
physician for their diagnosis. At home, we thank
the kids for being obedient. We even thank our
spouse for their kind gestures and
everyday thoughtfulness.

Of all the *"Thanks"* given, throughout the entire
day, Christ is often the least thanked and the most
deserving. Today is the day that He has made. He
has given us His air, His earth, His sovereignty,
and His grace. We should give Him our thanks.
In all that you do today, remember,
every good thing is from Him.
Bless God today with your thanks!

Thank You

For every time I scraped my knee,
that You were there to comfort me,
I say, "thank you" now.
For the many years You gave me Your best
and for honoring my selfishly made request,
I say, "thank you" now.
For not leaving me when my life looked grim,
for wiping my tears and for increasing my strength.
For giving unto me the words of prayer;
for being God over the sea, land, and the air,
I say, "thank you" now.
For the nights that I slept worry free,
because intercessors were praying for me;
for the many things of days gone by,
that have been entrusted to me, then and now.
For teaching me courage and extending me grace;
for developing my character and elevating my faith,
I say, "thank you" now.

Times Past

"Personal Praise Page"

I thank you for each day I live
worry free. I thank you for standing
by me when no one else would. I
thank you for your unconditional
love. I thank Jesus for my family's
my friends. I thank him for my
negative test results. Most of all
I thank Jesus just for loving me
the way he has and never giving
up on me, even when I had
given up on me and of his
love.

Today's Power Phrase

Don't Overlook

The Small Stuff

When You Do

It Grows Into

The Big Stuff

Times Past

Day 3

*Therefore my heart is glad and my tongue rejoices;
my body also will rest secure.
(Psalms 16:9)*

Some days you must focus on the small things so that you can believe in the bigger things that are yet to come.

One *"thank you"* must represent the thousand that went unheard. One call, letter, touch, or one friend, must represent all of those you may have been expecting.

If you can see life's *small* delights, you will find them *enlarged* as you continue to look on. Like the sun that brightens an entire continent, or a star that illuminates in darkness, the *small* things have always made the biggest differences.

Allow *hope* to do that for you today. A *tiny* bit of hope is all you really need.

If you hold on, you will find your hope is about to produce a great big wonder in your life.

All things become possible when you believe!

A Ray of Hope

Only God knows what you go through.
He is the only one who knows your pain.
When there is nothing else anyone can do,
nor fix, mend, or change,
He seeks to send "A Ray of Hope,"
but some think hope is a dream.
He seeks to show you once again
how things are better than they seem.

Yesterday, what the world did not know,
and what they could not conceive
will tomorrow become a miracle,
that He'll open their eyes to see.
Today, take the time to reflect
on the works of the Creator's hands,
He's about to reveal what you have believed:
"that it is all working according to plan."

Times Past

"Personal Praise Page"

_____

_____

_____

_____

_____

_____

_____

_____

_____

_____

_____

_____

_____

_____

Today's Power Phrase

If God Is

In Your Plans

You Have Nothing

To Worry About

Times Past

Day 4

May the words of my mouth
and the meditation of my heart
be pleasing in your sight,
O Lord, my Rock and my Redeemer.
(Psalms 19:14)

What a schedule!
The meetings are planned.
The trips are arranged.
Last minute items are all firmed up.
But is everything noted?

A day-timer, a secretary, and a palm pilot, but
something (someone) is still missing
from your agenda.
His name is not found anywhere in your schedule.
Appointments are there! Lunch is there!
Even those things you deemed *"unimportant"*
are there, but He seems to be missing.

Our schedules and daily agendas are
filled with so many tasks and events that it
appears very little room is left for Him.
God is looking for His place in your day,
your week, your plans,...your life.
It is still not too late to allow Him in.

God's Agenda

God has saved us from a world of sin.
What a mess our lives had been!
And we have done all but remember
to put Him somewhere on our agenda.

God has been there when we lost our hope.
He untangled the knots of satan's rope.
And why did He not allow us to surrender?
Because He had us on His agenda.

He has picked us up, time after time;
even though we have let Him down.
So, why is it so hard for us to render
a place for God on our agenda?

God has gone to prepare a place for us.
He has made room for us all to enter.
He is looking for our place for Him
somewhere on our agenda.

Times Past

"Personal Praise Page"

_____

_____

_____

_____

_____

_____

_____

_____

_____

_____

_____

_____

_____

_____

Today's Power Phrase

Success Is

Boldly Going

Where God Always

Knew You Could

Times Past

Day 5

Even though I walk through the valley...
I will fear no evil, for you are with me;
your rod and your staff they comfort me.
(Psalms 23:4)

When you reach your destiny you will say,
"I didn't mind the trip."

Today, you are in a destination
en route to your destiny.
It may not be a place of pleasure,
but it is an atmosphere where learning takes place
and your growth is revealed and developed.

Take heart in knowing that God has
predestined your triumphant finish.

So when you have come to
an unpleasant destination
along your way, remember that
your current destination
is not your final destiny.

Continue along life's journey.
Embrace His plan and watch how you grow!

Life's Journey

When life makes you feel that you just cannot have
all that your heart desires,
God wants you to know that within your reach
are all the things He will help you acquire.

When you are traveling along and are feeling life's pains,
it's your blessing the devil is after!
Trust in the Father and press through the pain,
let your faith look up to the Master!

When you feel that life has dealt you an unfair hand,
and you know that you are falling, but not where you will land.
Remember this journey that we all travel on,
will only be finished if we continue along.

For only in life can you follow a dream,
find faith, have failures, yet still believe.
And what you will find if you do not give in,
is that all of the winners rejoice at the end.

Times Past

"Personal Praise Page"

_____

_____

_____

_____

_____

_____

_____

_____

_____

_____

_____

_____

_____

Today's Power Phrase

God Only

Requires

You To Use

What You Have

Times Past

Day 6

What is man that you are mindful of him...
(Psalms 8:4)

Today we should take a lesson from some of God's other creations to see if they are struggling to do what He designed them to do.

Have you ever noticed that the bird does not seem to have a problem flying? The dog does not seem to have a problem barking. The cat seems to have no problem purring. Fish seem to be content swimming. Frogs have not stopped jumping. Rain does not have a problem falling. And the sun seems to get right in place and shine.
Doesn't it make you wonder how it is that the rest of God's creations are doing exactly what they were created to do?
How about you?

God was so mindful of us that He gave us rule over the land, sea, and every creepy, crawly thing. Therefore, we should be even more focused on what He has created us to do,
becoming what He intended us to be.
Today when you look at one of God's creations and marvel, just imagine how they
must look at *You*.

You Can

You can smile when the sun is farthest.
You can laugh when the day turns grim.
Understand, every rain has its beginning;
and every beginning has a date with its end.

You can sing when your heart is not in it.
You can dance though your shoes are worn out.
God wants you caught up in praise,
because you do not see Him while you pout.

You are not alone, though you feel lonely.
You can make it, though you are feeling dismayed.
God has been with you since the beginning,
and He will be with you til the end of the age.

Times Past

"Personal Praise Page"

_____

_____

_____

_____

_____

_____

_____

_____

_____

_____

_____

_____

_____

_____

_____

Today's Power Phrase

The Promises

Of God

Are Better Than Sure

They Are

Guaranteed

Times Past

Day 7

The lions may grow weak and hungry,
but those who seek the Lord lack no good thing.
(Psalms 34:10)

Some days you cannot see how much
you have grown.
But you have grown, regardless of what the
adversary says!
You cannot always measure growth
with the natural eye.
Sometimes growth takes a different route.
When other people are looking for growth's height,
God is growing your roots.
Roots are important, you know?
You need deep roots to keep you
from being tossed by every wind of emotion.
You need deep roots to keep you from reacting to
every disappointment.

He is growing you!

The Master is lovingly, gently,
artistically, growing you.
So whether He is growing your roots
or growing you up,
don't fight the growing!

28

Keep Growing

In the spirit, if you looked, you would clearly see,
how the Father is at work; He is growing me!
Trials are merely inches on the Master's growing scale;
tests are future testimonies I have yet to tell.
I must continue onward, I must follow where He leads.
He alone can take me places, even I have never dreamed.
If I abide with the Father,
He said, that He would abide with me.
It is He who knows my future,
He has planned my destiny.
He said, I would surely prosper.
He said, that I would succeed.
He has given me a hope,
that hope has quickened my belief.
So I must focus on my finish,
for at the winner's gate will be,
the Alpha & Omega, standing -- waiting just for me.

Times Past

"Personal Praise Page"

_____

_____

_____

_____

_____

_____

_____

_____

_____

_____

_____

_____

_____

_____

Today's Power Phrase

Faith

Follows

The Father

Fearlessly

Times Past

Day 8

*I desire to do your will, O my God;
your law is within my heart.
(Psalms 40:8)*

Today is a good day to do something better than
you did yesterday, kinder than last week, and
more generous than last year.
Today is a good day to do exactly what you have
always said,
"you would do differently next time."
I encourage you to be the first to say,
"hello" today.
I encourage you to *smile* at someone you don't
know today.
I encourage you to do *something* today that will
absolutely bless someone else's life.
If you do, you will find, when the day is done,
you will have blessed your own life as well.

Have an awesome day!

Do It Different Today

How many times have I said, "no"
when I could have just said, "yes"?
How many times have I committed myself
and just didn't give it my best?
There were times I just could have taken a moment,
but at the time it seemed too much.
There were so many promises made, that were broken,
in the lives of people I have touched.
I hid though I knew you needed my help.
I had ideas I knew you could use.
But I was not standing where I thought you could see me,
because I knew it would be me that you would choose.
I saw in your face that you were grieving;
I did not try to understand.
Many times I knew you were struggling,
and I chose not to lend you a hand.
I received the message you wanted to see me,
how important it was that I call;
I just did not think it important enough,
so I didn't respond at all.
Yesterday has come and gone,
and as I sit now and reminisce,
I find so many wonderful things I had done,
are shadowed by those that I missed.

Times Past

"Personal Praise Page"

_____

_____

_____

_____

_____

_____

_____

_____

_____

_____

_____

_____

_____

_____

_____

_____

_____

Today's Power Phrase

Hope's Greatest

Reward

Is Having Seen

It's Testimony

Come To

Pass

Times Past

Day 9

*Guide me in your truth and teach me, for you are God
my Savior, and my hope is in you all day long.
(Psalms 25:5)*

Someone sadly -- quietly -- drifted into
eternity last night.
They were probably unaware that yesterday
would be their last chance to do whatever...,
their last day to say what mattered. Yesterday,
they undoubtedly could not imagine that they
would not see the day break ever again.

But we have today!

Today we realize that yesterday's greatest pains
did not overtake us. Today we realize that
yesterday's disappointments did not crush us.
Today we realize that the lessons learned
yesterday did not destroy us.

We are still standing!

Today's grace cannot be wasted, nor can today's
opportunities. For if you live today you see
today's glory – today's splendor.
For today is all we have for sure.
Live Today!

Daybreak Once Again

I smile to see the daybreak once again,
the glow that gently wakes me from the night.
A brand new day, in which I have never been--
I am awed to see the newness of the light.
The clouds have passed, the sun begins to shine,
although there is still a mist in the air.
Another day God has given to be mine,
and I can feel His presence everywhere.

I dare to go about this day alone.
What fate, before me, shall each hour meet?
I know my life is His. I'm not my own.
All to Him I owe, this sinner's soul He keeps.

Time passes fast -- the sun and all it's light
fades away as day turns into night.
Hope is restored in rest, and strength is regained.
My prayer is to see daybreak once again.

Times Past

"Personal Praise Page"

_____

_____

_____

_____

_____

_____

_____

_____

_____

_____

_____

_____

_____

_____

Today's Power Phrase

There Is

No Better Day

Than Today And

No Better Hour

Than Now

Times Past

Day 10

This is the day the Lord has made;
let us rejoice and be glad in it.
(Psalms 118:24)

Have you ever been mistakenly associated with
someone else? Maybe you have.
There are at least three enemies that try to
associate themselves with you:
"Wish I Had," "I Think I Can,"
and *"Glad I Tried."*

Do they sound familiar?

These people are not good enough to even be in
your circle!
The only people whose name should be mentioned
alongside yours is *"Can Do."*
That's right, *"Can Do,"* because you *"Can Do"*
all things through Him who gives you strength.

Today, look for ways to do something
that the other three <u>would not</u> do,
and thought you would not do either.

Today is your day to prove them wrong!

One of the Three

"Wish I Had" complained and grumbled
quite an awful lot.
He never seemed to be satisfied
with the little that he got.
"I think I Can" became someone
not many understood.
He rarely did the many things
he often said he could.
"Glad I Tried" took a chance
but never reached his goal.
He proclaimed, "at least I tried,"
in his years of old.
But "Can Do" kept striving
to be the best that he could be,
in spite of the many obstacles
that he could not foresee.
Each of them had the potential
to do great and wondrous things,
but "Can Do" found out
that those who Do - achieve.

Times Past

"Personal Praise Page"

_____

_____

_____

_____

_____

_____

_____

_____

_____

_____

_____

_____

_____

_____

_____

Today's Power Phrase

Expect His Favor

To Go Before You

Tearing Down Walls

And

Opening

Doors

Times Past

Day 11

May the favor of the Lord our God
rest upon us; establish the work of our hands
for us-yes, establish the work of our hands.
(Psalms 90:17)

The one divine characteristic that we can use
more of is:
"Courage."
You do not need worldly arrogance when you have
"Godly Courage."
The God kind of Courage urges you to be quiet
when your flesh wants to speak out.
The God kind of Courage allows you to speak with
"Holy Boldness" when all common sense
says it will cost you to speak.
(The truth is, it will cost you if you don't!)
The God kind of Courage understands
that timing is everything.
God's Timing is Everything!
Premature boldness, is oftentimes arrogance,
mistaken for courage.

Today pray for your courage to come alive.
Pray that you listen to its prompting.
Pray that you respond.

COURAGE

Carefully guide me so that I can see the shrapnel in the road.

Open my mind, Lord, to the "Book" where the greatest stories are told.

Undergird my faith so that my enemies do not prevail.

Ready my heart for battle, do not let my faith fail.

Allow only good seed to proceed out of my hand.

Guard my thoughts from thinking things that are not a part of your plan.

Engulf my spirit with purpose — purpose me to greater works.
Call me not to heaven, until all my work is done on earth.

Times Past

"Personal Praise Page"

_____

_____

_____

_____

_____

_____

_____

_____

_____

_____

_____

_____

_____

_____

_____

_____

Today's Power Phrase

A Friend

Loves You

Through

Everything

Times Past

Day 12

I am a friend to all who fear you,
to all who follow your precepts.
(Psalms 119:63)

Celebrate your friendships today!

Every friend has not stabbed you in the back.
Every friendship has not failed.
Every friend has not betrayed you.
Some friendships are still worth saving.
Remember those today who have challenged you
to do better, encouraged you to
follow your dreams,
and even supported your crazy ideas.
Celebrate friendships today!
Celebrate the friends who have made you laugh,
those who have imparted unto you wisdom,
and those who have taught you things you could
not have learned in books.
Celebrate those friendships today!

Reach out to friendships today.
Reach out to an old friend –
and reach out for a new one!

My Friend

Your love reached out to me,
even when you did not understand.
Your arms embraced me,
and you gently eased my pains.
You saw my faults,
but you did not tear me down.
You helped build my faith
and it has turned my whole world around.
You always notice the good I try to do.
The best in me, naturally comes out when I'm with you.
In my sorrows you believed that I would rise again.
In my triumphs, you were there just to hold my hand.
Like a gem,
you have lasted through the thick and thin.
Tell me, how do I give back
to you, My Friend?

Times Past

"Personal Praise Page"

_____

_____

_____

_____

_____

_____

_____

_____

_____

_____

_____

_____

_____

_____

Today's Power Phrase

The Mirror

Only Reflects

The Image

It Sees

Times Past

Day 13

Ascribe to the Lord, O mighty ones,
ascribe to the Lord glory and strength.
(Psalms 29:1)

To look like Christ...
To love like Christ...
To be like Christ...

The Christian walk is not easy, but it is attainable.
In my best efforts I falter,
but I cannot kick myself.
I must continue daily, to submit myself to the
Master's cry.

When I hear Him today, I will answer.
What He speaks today, I will obey.
If I fail, it is He who encourages me to
get up, shake the dust off my failures
and continue to walk in His will.

I become bigger, better, greater,
and mightier because I respond
when the Master calls.

Today, listen for Him. When He calls you, respond:
"Speak Lord, for your servant heareth."

A Mighty Christian

Who will answer, "yes" to the Master's cry?
A mighty Christian is he!
Whose life is the example that shows the world how
a Godly person's should be?
Who is worthy to be called the King's child?
A mighty Christian is he!
Whose might is not measured by the title he holds
but by a work that all can see?

Who has been tempted, tried, and persecuted,
yet stands victorious?
It is he who can triumph when he seeks God in prayer
and finds that His strength is enough.

When the Master looks at the world
what is it that He sees?

Is it a people with selfish ambitions?
Is it a people who longs after thee?

For those who are His, He has destined;
with His blood they have been justified.
And by name He has marked the Christians
who will answer the Master's cry.

Times Past

"Personal Praise Page"

_____

_____

_____

_____

_____

_____

_____

_____

_____

_____

_____

_____

_____

Today's Power Phrase

No

Heavenly Battle

Is Ever Lost

To The devil

Times Past

Day 14

The fear of the Lord is the beginning of wisdom;
all who follow his precepts have good understanding.
To him belongs eternal praise.
(Psalms 111:10)

Some things appear unfair.
The door you thought would open is closed.
The help you thought was coming has not arrived.
The people who promised to be with you are gone.

But you are not defeated!

Being defeated does not depend on people,
promises, or things in your life.
Defeat depends on you!

You cannot concede!

Defeat is not an option!
Losing is not an option!
Giving in, giving up, and/or giving back
are not options!

"You Must Continue To Follow Him!"

I Will Follow

Sometimes I cannot see the way in which I need to go;
yet, I do want to go the path, in which I am to grow.

It seems each corner that I turn, there stands another wall;
but I alone cannot bring them down, they just refuse to fall.

The path I am to travel, Lord, I leave it up to You;
remove the things that block the work You have called on me to do.

The challenges I am faced with — as enormous as they appear
are not just mine to carry, since the heavy loads You share.

You promised that I would have no more on me than I could bear;
so the burden is not my worry. You have taught me well how to not fear.

Since you are Father -- and the author of my life and destiny,
today I step aside, and I will follow where you lead.

Times Past

"Personal Praise Page"

_____

_____

_____

_____

_____

_____

_____

_____

_____

_____

_____

_____

_____

_____

_____

_____

Today's Power Phrase

Worship Is Our

Weapon In Warfare

That Helps Us

To Win

Times Past

Day 15

Blessed are the people of whom this is true;
blessed are the people whose God is the Lord.
(Psalms 144:15)

Complaining has not gotten anyone anywhere.
You have tried it. I have tried it. We have all
mastered it, but we have been unsuccessful
at achieving anything by it.
It is just not as effective as we would like to
believe.
Everyone around already knows what is broken.
(It has been previously reported.)
Who is willing to be part of the solution?
If you cannot do anything about today's situation,
refuse to complain about it today.
If it is beyond your ability to fix it, change it,
or correct it, use your God-given authority to
pray about it until it does change.
What is important today is
realizing what you **CAN** do.
There is no doubt about it,
prayer is something we all can do!!
In the strains and stresses of our day, while
realizing the limits of our natural abilities, we have
an assurance that God **will do**
those things that we cannot.

60

When the Load Seems Too Heavy

God watches over all of us;
He sees and yes, He cares.
He knows sometimes we feel the load
is much too hard to bear.

He loves us enough to keep us,
in our moments of despair;
He is our present help.
He is always near.

He holds us up and comforts us
through heartaches and through tears.
If we take our burdens to Him
we must trust and leave them there.

He is the one who gave His life
to make us joint heirs.
He wants us to give our load
to Him in prayer.

Times Past

"Personal Praise Page"

_____

_____

_____

_____

_____

_____

_____

_____

_____

_____

_____

_____

_____

_____

Today's Power Phrase

His Rest

Is His Reward

For Work

Well-done

Times Past

Day 16

Today, if you hear his voice,
do not harden your hearts...
(Psalms 95:7-8)

Yesterday, there were many things I said
I would not do.
I was not going to let the boss get to me.
I was not going to lose my cool.
I was not going to comment on every situation.
I was not going to focus on getting the last word.

Yesterday, I said I was going to do some things
differently:
I was going to be the first to apologize.
I was going to help someone who did not ask.
I was going to do something kind
without being found out.
I was going to reach out, with the love of Christ
and touch someone else's life.

Yesterday, I thought I had good intentions.

Today, I realize that *good* intentions
are not *good* at all, unless
the *good* is accomplished.

Another Day Gone By

Another day has come and gone,
what is left are the memories.
Each day past has been filled with hopes
and possibilities.
But each yesterday is lost to time
and can never be regained.
The past belongs to history
and is not to be reclaimed.
Today offers though, another chance
to start a fresh — anew,
to take a look at all you have done
and all you would like to do.
But unless you take advantage
of each moment in its time,
tomorrow you will awake to find
another day has gone by.

Times Past

"Personal Praise Page"

_____

_____

_____

_____

_____

_____

_____

_____

_____

_____

_____

_____

_____

Today's Power Phrase

His Power

Can Be

Released

Through Prayer

Times Past

Praise be to God, who has not rejected
my prayer or withheld his love from me!
(Psalms 66:20)

It is funny how quickly we can forget
the fundamentals of our strength.
Remember the day we started off in prayer?
That was a good day!
Our prayers were heard. Our prayers were
answered, and our enemies behaved.
It's the power of prayer!
Throughout the month, prayer has become
something *sandwiched* between our problems and
our situations.
We have missed many opportunities for
Thanksgiving.
It is at the beginning of anything that we are more
likely to be focused on prayer. But we must
remember that the essential ingredient to our
successful day, week, month, and year is
our continual prayer.
Today, remember to seek God
before attempting to do anything.
Today, remember to pray first
and strive to remain in an attitude of prayer
all day long.

Daily Prayer

Father, in Heaven once again, I lift my heart to thee;
today I have come to ask you, Lord, for only what I need.
Take away my imperfections; make me all anew.
Take me and hold me, shape me and mold me,
I want to be more like You.
Let all of the problems I am faced with today,
not come in such disarray.
If I am unable to face them alone
be there to show me the way.
If I am tempted and tried by my enemies
do not let it show on my face.
Do not let my pressures seem more than they are,
make my load lighter today.
Today let me be all that I can
and let all of Your goodness shine through.
Let me not feel the stress or the strain
in the things that I know I must do.
Teach me, dear Lord, to walk with grace.
Help me to not go astray.
And as I approach each brand new day
remind me to start off in prayer.

Times Past

"Personal Praise Page"

_____

_____

_____

_____

_____

_____

_____

_____

_____

_____

_____

_____

_____

_____

_____

Today's Power Phrase

You Will Do Nothing

By Chance

And Everything By

Divine

Providence

Times Past

Day 18

You know when I sit and when I rise;
you perceive my thoughts from afar.
(Psalms 139:2)

Nothing is coincidental!
The illusion of coincidence is error.
Your meeting with a certain person at a particular
time is not coincidental.
Your getting the job is not by chance.
You did not just *happen* to be in the right place
at the right time.
God has gone through an awesome planning
process on your behalf.
His plans for you are not manifesting themselves
by chance.
He has planned for you to walk in health.
He has planned for you to walk in prosperity.
He has planned for you to walk in favor.
No, it is not coming to pass by chance!
It is coming to pass by divine planning.
What seems coincidental is purposed.
What looks like chance is the conscious work
of the Eternal, interceding for your good.

Celebrate His forethought of You!

De-Ja-Vu

I awoke early this morning,
feeling I was still in a dream.

My thoughts of the Father so prevalent
I wondered, what it could mean?

It was His face that I felt near me.
My heart was engulfed by His touch.

Then, with a sudden awakening,
I arose in sort of a rush.

Was it the smell in the room or a memory?
Was it His fragrance? I thought I knew.

For a moment my earth and His heaven were one
Now I ask, "God, was it really you?"

In this world many believe things just happen,
they say it is fate, and some think it chance.

But my thoughts of you on this morning
was not mere coincidence.

Times Past

"Personal Praise Page"

_____

_____

_____

_____

_____

_____

_____

_____

_____

_____

_____

_____

_____

_____

Today's Power Phrase

You Don't Have

To Be

Famous To Be

Unforgettable

Times Past

Day 19

Satisfy us in the morning with your unfailing love,
that we may sing for joy and be glad all our days.
(Psalms 90:14)

Some people don't know how significant
they are in your life.
Some people do not apprehend how much
their smile brightens your day.
Some people cannot comprehend how much of an
encouragement they have been.
What others bring to your life cannot be
measured, but it can be expressed from the
heartfelt appreciation you choose to share.
Tell your Pastor...
Tell your co-workers...
Tell your friends...
Tell someone special in your life **today**
how important their relationship is to you.

Creed

There will be times you will forget all you pledged to share.
There will be days you will fail to take the time
to earnestly show you care.
There will be times when you will remember things you promised to
forget.
There will be days you are filled with anger and say some things
you will regret.
There will be times when saying sorry will be a word that just won't
do.
There will be days when you will not hear a single soul say,
"I love you."
There will be times it is hard to fix it.
There will be days your heart is not in it.
So today, just take a minute, tell someone
how rich your life is because they are in it.
There will be times when you want to talk and just want
someone to listen.
There will be days that you will try, but fail, to make the right
decision.
There will be times you will not see things quite the way others do.
There will be days when someone is up late praying just for you.
There will be times when you will think the worst has surely come.
There will be days when you will feel that the enemy has won.
There will be times when you will not show it,
and days you will expect others just to know it.
But today, take a minute, tell someone,
how rich your life is because they are in it.

Times Past

"Personal Praise Page"

_____

_____

_____

_____

_____

_____

_____

_____

_____

_____

_____

_____

_____

_____

_____

Today's Power Phrase

Life Lessons

Are Many Times

The

Greatest

Teachers

Times Past

Day 20

I will instruct you and teach you in the way you should go;
I will counsel you and watch over you.
(Psalms 32:8)

I could quit,
but no one would know that
I possess the spirit of a finisher.
I could scream,
but those who would hear me
might think I'm crazy.
I could pout,
but I would just be accused of acting like a baby.
I could retaliate,
but then I would be perceived as being vindictive.
I could do what the enemy expects me to do,
but that would not give testimony to God.

Today, God has left the choice of what <u>I will do</u>
up to me.

Making the Difference

That we would take upon ourselves to see another's need,

seek to find a way to help, by some small word or deed.

That we make a vow -- a promise -- to never let it be,

that someone crossed our path today we did not even see.

But in every opportunity, may we strive to lend a hand,

so that a sister or a brother can see the making of a friend.

For as we try to make a difference in the lives of others,

we soon will see how very much we all need one another.

Times Past

"Personal Praise Page"

_____

_____

_____

_____

_____

_____

_____

_____

_____

_____

_____

_____

_____

Today's Power Phrase

Blessings Are

Looking For You

They've Got Your

Name On Them

Times Past

Day 21

You are the most excellent of men and your lips have been anointed with grace, since God has blessed you forever.
(Psalms 45:2)

Guard your ears, your eyes, and your heart,
so that you do not miss the blessing.
Sometimes what you *see* is not always what it
appears to be.
Get the facts! Do not react on feelings.
Do not allow negativity to overtake your day.
Negativity is a *spirit* and spirits transfer.
The eyes are the windows to the soul.
The heart is your life source; guard it!
Everyone cannot hold your heart in their hands.
Choose your friends, acquaintances,
and associates well.
Be selective! Be specific! Be sure!
Today is your day.
The body will only recognize what you
allow it to see, hear, and feel.
All around you are blessings to be seen, and
regardless of what you hear, how it looks, or feels,
if you are not careful you may fail to count a
wonderful blessing in your today.
They are there! Dare to count them!

The Ones You Didn't Count

Those things we cannot measure
by dollars nor by cents.
Those things we take for granted,
like our daily health and strength.
The cost we do not tally
as each day we travel on
are treasures which we find rarely spoken of.
Those things we don't remember
from one moment to the next:
the tragedies we have evaded,
the accidents we have escaped.
Those things we do not earn
but somehow seem to get,
those things we are simply given;
all of which are heaven sent.
The love that we are shown
down throughout the years;
the friends that we have made,
the grief that we have been spared.
If you add up all your blessings
some you probably would leave out,
and the greatest of them all
would be the ones you did not count.

Times Past

"Personal Praise Page"

_____

_____

_____

_____

_____

_____

_____

_____

_____

_____

_____

_____

_____

Today's Power Phrase

God's View

Is Best

Since He Can See It All

Trust Him To

Handle It

All

Times Past

Day 22

*From heaven the Lord looks down and sees all mankind;
from his dwelling place he watches all who live on earth.
(Psalms 33:13-14)*

Recognizing what is around you is important.
If you cannot recognize what is around you,
you cannot lean, when you need to,
on the help that is near you.
The help you need is very present today.
Everywhere you will go, He is there waiting for you
to lean. He is present in your situation waiting
for you to call on Him.
Your help is watching over you today.
And even if you do not acknowledge Him, He will
be the one who catches you before you fall.
He will lift you up, hold your hand, and make
sure that you get right back in place and
continue on.

You Are Everywhere

Everywhere I will go You have been.
Everything I will see You have seen.
I need never seek to find something new
if I simply continue to follow You.

Everything I will say, You have heard.
Everything that is taught You have learned.
Everything I will hear has been said,
spoken from a thought You have had.

I would find it to my benefit
to go where You prefer I went,
for wisdom found while here on earth
was divinely planned before my birth.

Times Past

"Personal Praise Page"

_____

_____

_____

_____

_____

_____

_____

_____

_____

_____

_____

_____

_____

_____

Today's Power Phrase

To Encourage

Someone Today

Is To Touch

The Heart

Of God

Today

Times Past

Day 23

You hear, O Lord, the desire of the afflicted;
you encourage them, and you listen to their cry.
(Psalms 10:17)

The thing we all need the most may be
the thing we receive the least.

When you are challenged with temptations,
test, and trials, you need encouragement.
Daily you face, seemingly, overwhelming issues.
Daily you are challenged to be light
in a dark world.
Encouragement should take place like meals,
three times a day (minimum).
You need to be encouraged today because
someone needs encouragement from you today.

A few years ago the Lord challenged me to do
something I thought was crazy. He told me I
would find encouragement simply by encouraging
the lives of others.

Can you believe that?
Did I believe that?
I challenge you today to try it.
Your very own encouragement is in your hands!

What Encourages Me

Everyone can use encouragement,
a lift along the way;
a pick me up when you are feeling low,
when bluish skies turn gray.
A word or phrase — some compassion,
that is heartfelt and sincere;
that brightens up a gloomy day,
turning dreariness into cheer.
Every now and then
we all get a little down,
and there is nothing like encouragement
to turn things all around.
To show a brighter side -
a different point of view;
that is what encouragement
always strives to do.
Sometimes it is a little note
that simply says, "I care."
Sometimes it is letting someone know
that you will always be there.
But the reward that comes from encouragement,
as simple as it may be;
it is knowing I have encouraged you.
That is what encourages me!!

Times Past

"Personal Praise Page"

_____

_____

_____

_____

_____

_____

_____

_____

_____

_____

_____

_____

_____

Today's Power Phrase

Because Of

Christ

The devil

Has Everything

To Fear Today

Times Past

Day 24

*Though you have made me see troubles,
many and bitter, you will restore my life
again; from the depths of the earth you will
again bring me up.
(Psalms 71:20)*

Either we get use to the idea of repeating lessons
in life or we have not gotten sick and tired of
being sick and tired of repeating them.

We do not have to continue going this way.

The route we took yesterday, if taken today, will
lead us to the same place.

If that is not where you want to end up,
then you must take a different route.

Tomorrow you will either look forward
to something new or dread doing the same thing
all over again.

Here We Go Again

Back and forth -- up and down,
that is where we seem to go.
Why we fight so hard to learn?
I guess we will never know.
High or low -- good or bad,
somewhere our feelings lie.
And every time we reach the bottom
we give it one more try.
Is it yes or no, is it right or wrong?
There is no in-between.
We do not compromise
because we know not what that means.
It was all for me, or all for us;
that was yesterday.
Now it is all for the one who gets it first,
that is how we think today.
It is breaking up and making up,
but no one ever wins.
It is not knowing when we have had enough,
so, here we go again.

Times Past

"Personal Praise Page"

_____

_____

_____

_____

_____

_____

_____

_____

_____

_____

_____

_____

_____

_____

Today's Power Phrase

Praise

Is The

Melody

That

Prayer

Brings

Times Past

Day 25

By day the Lord directs his love,
at night his song is with me — a
prayer to the God of my life.
(Psalms 42:8)

There is no such thing as praying too early,
too late, too little, or too much.

Prayer is your communication key:
the key to the lives of people you do not know,
and the key to situations you cannot change.
It is the tool that gives you the power to
invoke the change that you want to see.
Prayer is your best defense against the enemy,
the best option when indecisive,
the best solution to any problem you face.
In prayer you can celebrate, request,
intercede, and receive.
It can be public, private, corporate, or individual.
It is God's way of keeping your relationship fresh,
interesting, and challenging.
It is your way to get His attention.

Make It A Matter of Prayer

The goals that you have, those things that you dream,
the impossible task that you dare,
take them to God for the guidance you need,
make it a matter of prayer.
The pressures in life that you face day to day,
when you are troubled by thoughts and by cares;
He who knows all will deliver you through
when you make it a matter of prayer.
When you are alone, no friend to be found,
no one you have called on is there.
Call Him on high, He will come through on time,
when you make it a matter of prayer.
All trials and tests, that we all must face,
at times may seem unfair;
but God only gives what He knows we can take,
when we make it a matter of prayer.
The prize we shall win when this life is done,
our reward for all of the tears,
becomes possible if we trust and have faith,
to make it a matter of prayer.

Times Past

"Personal Praise Page"

_____

_____

_____

_____

_____

_____

_____

_____

_____

_____

_____

_____

_____

_____

_____

Today's Power Phrase

Evidence

Of His Love

Is

Everywhere

You Turn

Times Past

Day 26

It was not by their sword that they won the land,
nor did their arm bring them victory; it was your
right hand, your arm, and the light of your face,
for you loved them.
(Psalms 44:3)

Today is "Hug Day" for you.
Yes, "Hug Day."
Give yourself a Hug today!
For as often as you receive one of
those hugs that screams
"I really do not want to do this,"
you need to reach
into your uttermost and find
Heaven's Hug that resides within you.
Then sincerely, wrap your arms
around yourself and squeeze tight.

Children should not leave the house without hugs!

Spouses should not leave the house without hugs!

You should not leave the house without a hug!

Celebrate Hug Day!

Hugs To You

Hugs are so important,
it is an expression of our care.
We can give them and receive them,
yet still have more to share.

Hugs that are earnest in our sorrow,
and those that are dearest in our pain,
we remember long, long after our
zapped strength has been regained.

Hugs are available in our triumphs,
celebrating our times of joy;
all of them we must savor,
for in the heart true hugs are stored.

So hugs can never be depleted,
for in the place where hugs reside,
is an endless hug from heaven
found within you, deep inside.

Times Past

"Personal Praise Page"

Today's Power Phrase

I Am My

Absolute Best

When I Let Go

And Let God

Times Past

Day 27

Many are asking, "Who can show us any good?"
Let the light of your face shine upon us, O Lord.
(Psalms 4:6)

There are some days when you do not
feel like smiling.
There are days you do not want to submit to
anyone, or do the good you know to do.
There are days when you would rather retaliate
and take your own revenge.

But you have been chosen to do good even when
you don't want to. You have been given God's
measure of grace which is sufficient to keep you.
He has entrusted you to "light" the world with
the character traits of Christ.

It's a tough job, but He chose you because
He knew your life would give Him
glory, honor, and praise.

Do not stop being "A Good Christian."

A Good Christian

Must I try to be an example to everyone I meet?
Must I love the unknown man that I pass by on the street?
Must I always forgive my enemies, even the ones who seem not to care?
Must I humble myself in a no-win situation even if it seems unfair?
Must I give a hand to the needy, when I am needing a hand for
myself?
Must I give the last of what I have, or share it with someone else?
If a stranger comes to the door, is it wise that I let him in?
Since I, too, once was a stranger that You chose to befriend.

My heart belongs to You, dear Lord. Fill it up with what is missing.
Give me the heart of a righteous man. Teach me to be a good Christian.

If I must go the extra mile for someone, or do an anonymous deed,
I am here so that You can use me Lord, wherever You see the need.
Since You know what I can accomplish,
the things I can and cannot do,
that which You chose for me and my life,
I am leaving it all up to You.
So each day as I am in Your light, striving with the best of intentions,
let others see when they are looking at me,
that I desire to be "A Good Christian."

Times Past

"Personal Praise Page"

_____

_____

_____

_____

_____

_____

_____

_____

_____

_____

_____

_____

_____

Today's Power Phrase

Your Position

Is Secure

When You Are

Securely Positioned

In Him

Times Past

Day 28

*You are my hiding place; you will protect me
from trouble and surround me with songs of deliverance.
(Psalms 32:7)*

You have tried to hide your tears,
but your eyes are watery and someone sees.
You have tried to hide your anger,
but your face is cold and someone sees.
You have tried to hide your feelings,
but your actions demonstrates something is
wrong, and someone sees.
You have been hiding in unsafe places, and
your hideouts have been exposed.

The God, who is the Rock,
sees your need for cover.
Today He covers you with love.
Today He covers you with understanding.
Today He covers you with strength to face those
from whom you have been trying to hide.
Allow Him to shield your emotions, cover your
disappointments, and love you through the day.
Step out of *hiding* and walk *boldly* today.
He has got you covered!

Hiding Place

I searched all over
just to find a hiding place;
but found instead
my hideouts have been quite unsafe.
Blindly I have sought refuge in
what seemed to be
a friend
until I found it was my enemy;
he was waiting to reveal where I had been --
he wanted to expose my hideout once again.
But one day I sought refuge in the Lord.
He was only after what was for my good.
Now I hide in Him, He keeps me safe,
surrounded by His love and by His grace.

Times Past

"Personal Praise Page"

_____

_____

_____

_____

_____

_____

_____

_____

_____

_____

_____

_____

_____

_____

Today's Power Phrase

Don't Let

Disappointment Drive You

You Have A

Destiny

To Pursue

Times Past

Day 29

Teach me, O Lord, to follow your decrees;
then I will keep them to the end.
(Psalms 119:33)

When you get to the end of a book
you want to find that it met your expectations
to the end.

When you finish a work day you want to
have accomplished something for your labor.

When you get to the end of your life you
want to have more to celebrate than regret.

Make today one of those days you will
rejoice about at the end.

At the End

Many things throughout today
we may not recognize.
Some things we call the devil's work,
are sent to us by God.
In troubles, heartache, strife and pain
you should always see
the hand of God reaching out
just to comfort thee.
So much we do not understand,
but Christ has faithfully
given men the greatest gift
the world has ever seen.
In this life His will and purpose
may not be understood.
Today, we just may fail to see
things working for our good.
But to give thanks is the act of faith
that says, "we trust God's plan is true,"
and at the end, God will prove
He's worked it out for you.

Times Past

"Personal Praise Page"

_____

_____

_____

_____

_____

_____

_____

_____

_____

_____

_____

_____

_____

_____

_____

_____

_____

_____

Today's Power Phrase

Some Things

Are Worth

Far More

Than Money

119

Times Past

Day 30

How priceless is your unfailing love! Both high and low among men find refuge in the shadow of your wings. (Psalms 36:7)

Love is an interesting thing.
Many people fail to see love, or give love because
of their distortion about what real love looks like.
The misconception about love has been based
upon romance novels and Hollywood movies.

We are not in a world where the truth
about love is hidden from us.
On the contrary, in the greatest book ever
written, (the one continuous "best seller"
throughout the ages,) you'll find love defined,
the unlovable justified, and the greatest example
of love, Jesus the Christ, was personified.
Love is waiting for you today.
So, reach up and receive more love than you
could ever comprehend in this life.
God's love shows the world a picture of what love
is suppose to look like.
Today, know that you are absolutely,
beyond a shadow of a doubt, loved.

The Father's Love

I cannot love you more than I already do,
I gave my best, in love, already.

I cannot hug you tighter than I already do,
without squeezing all life from inside of you.

I cannot hope for you more than I already do,
and you find "hope" more inviting.

I cannot share with you more than I already do,
when I share with you all that is exciting.

If you think about love as much as I do,
you would know that my loving was all about you;

in my thoughts, in my actions, and in all that I do
shows my unconditional love just for you!

My Son was my gift presented to you.
My best, in love, I have given you already.

Times Past

"Personal Praise Page"

_____

_____

_____

_____

_____

_____

_____

_____

_____

_____

_____

_____

_____

_____

_____

Today's Power Phrase

Everyday

Is Filled With

One Miracle

After

Another

Times Past

I will remember the deeds of the Lord; yes,
I will remember your miracles of long ago.
(Psalms 77:11)

There's nothing new under the sun.
What blessed you yesterday will bless you again.
What blessed you last week, last month, last year
are the same things that will bless you this week,
this month, and this year.
Everything you have faced is all you will face.
The devil is using the same tactics he used before.
Nothing new! Just a different day.
Let this monthly devotional bless you over,
and over, and over again.
Day One can do, again, what it did for you at the
beginning of this month, bless your day.
And when you find that you have come to the end
of another month, I hope you will have learned
more, overcome more, grown more, and stand
ready to begin with *Day One,* again.
I pray you never tire of a good daily dose of
encouragement.
And as you remember the best of "Times Past,"
remember, if you reach for the Psalms you can
rest in the Poetry, and grow in Power
through Prayer & Praise.
                                              -Theresa.

Remember

Every line within the "Book" contains a message.
Each word gives away a clue.
Every subject opens up a different forum,
and like an artist, where you begin, you are free to choose.
The message you read becomes the chisel — a carving tool;
what affects your heart depends upon what you are going through.

You become the Master's finest work — as your life gives Him praise.
This being His desire, for His best creation made.
As He looks back upon the writings --
His inspiration that men have put words to,
you will find that what's compiled is from His heart;
<u>This is His gift to You!</u>

"The Bible"

Times Past

"Personal Praise Page"

Other Books by Author

Mama Said Get in the House
(Embracing the Wisdom of Mama & God)
ISBN 0-9676710-0-0

"Mama Said, Get in the House"
delivers a message of wisdom and hope
through each inspirational page.
In chapter after chapter
one of Mama's principles is compared with the
same principle in Christendom.
You'll find within each line unfolds
an amazing woman's wisdom that was simply
wisdom from God.
It's your Mama's story.
It's my Mama's story,
It's every mother's story.
And it's when you laugh out loud
that you will have found your story
in the pages, and will have clearly given
yourself away.

Allen's Ink Publishing Company
P.O. Box 25099
Fayetteville, NC 28314

allens_ink@yahoo.com

Other Products By Author
Available Through

www.christianconnection.org

Cassettes, Videos and Books

Cassettes

Predestined to Be Conformed to His Likeness
She's Our Sister
Take Another Look
Will We Finish

Videos

Take Another Look
Will We Finish
She's Our Sister

Books

Mama Said, "Get in the House"
(Embracing the Wisdom of Mama & God)

For more information and/or pricelist, checkout our website or
e-mail us at: *products@christianconnection.org*
Or write us at: P.O. Box 25099
Fayetteville, NC 28314